The Resilient Missionary

The Resilient Missionary

THE LIFE STORY OF YOHANNES MENGSTEAB, A MISSIONARY TO AMERICA

Christine Schulden

ISBN: 0996677917
ISBN 13: 9780996677912
Library of Congress Control Number: 2015921315
Mission Nation Publishing Co., Naples, FL

Contents

Introductory Note from the Publisher

⌐

THE RESILIENT MISSIONARY IS THE first book in the Missionaries to America book series. The goal of the publisher, Mission Nation Publishing, is to "give a voice to missionaries to America," women and men who come to the United States to begin new gospel outreach.

As recorded in the New Testament, the church in Antioch was begun after the early Christians were driven out of Jerusalem upon the martyrdom of Saint Stephen; so today many Christians persecuted in their home countries have been forced to flee. Those who have found refuge in America have brought their faith with them.

Unfortunately, these refugees and immigrants are often looked down upon, seen as second-class ministers and citizens. Mission Nation Publishing seeks to show the courage, faith, and resilience of these gifts from God to the United States. Few stories demonstrate this more than the biography of Rev. Dr. Yohannes Mengsteab.

To find out more about the Missionaries to America, visit the website www.MissionNationPublishing.com. There you will find video interviews, books, and other resources to show the blessing that God is giving to America through these wonderful ministers of the gospel.

—Robert Scudieri, President, Mission Nation Publishing

From the Author

I'D LIKE TO THANK THE Lord, from whom all gifts and blessings are bestowed, for the honor to write this biography for Mission Nation. I'd like to also thank Mission Nation for entrusting me with the important task of telling Dr. Mengsteab's inspiring story. And, of course, I'd also like to thank my husband, John, and our three beautiful daughters, Hannah, Veronica, and Emily, for the courage, inspiration, and support to follow my dreams.

CHAPTER 1

War on the Horizon

THE GUN IN YOHANNES MENGSTEAB'S hands was heavy, and its weight seemed to increase as his fear of the impending war grew. With conflicting emotions struggling inside him, he settled under the sparkling stars, looking to validate his role in the fight that was about to begin. He felt heaven was being stingy with its answers. It seemed that all of his prayers yielded little guidance; the blinking stars above remained silent. Perhaps it wasn't that God was silent, but rather that Yohannes couldn't hear His words. Yohannes wished the stars spelled out words of inspiration, of divine council, of peace, but they only shed their cold light onto the arid landscape below. He set the burdensome gun beside him, got on his knees, bowed his head, and clasped his hands together tightly.

"Dear Lord," Yohannes prayed. "Please protect me during the battle we face tomorrow. I promise, Lord, if you spare me, I will serve You for the rest of my life. Please, Lord, let me live." Yohannes kept his eyes firmly closed, hoping to find an answer to his spiritual conflict—trying to spare himself the ridicule he'd endure should one of his comrades see the battle that was raging inside of him. Was he going to trust in guns or in God? In human leaders or in the Holy Spirit? He lay back on his spot on the ground, set the gun next to him with his hand fastened around the stock, and closed his eyes. His many Eritrean Liberation Front comrades surrounded him on the eve of the battle, but still he felt alone.

War had begun in Eritrea in 1977. Since 1961 Eritreans had been longing for independence from Ethiopia. The war in which Yohannes was fighting was just the most recent conflict in Eritrea's war-torn history. Italy had colonized Eritrea in 1890. Nearly fifty years later, the Italians invaded Eritrea's neighbor, Ethiopia, and claimed it too as part of their colonial empire—they called it "Italian East Africa."

After World War II, Ethiopia and Eritrea both became independent nations and were no longer controlled by Italy. But Eritreans enjoyed their independence only briefly. Ethiopia claimed Eritrea belonged to it, and a United Nations General Assembly agreed; Eritrea was made a part of Ethiopia.

In the late 1950s, a political movement began to organize in secret cells. Its goal was to regain Eritrea's independence. More and more Eritreans became disheartened with Ethiopian governance.

In July 1960 the Eritrean Liberation Front (ELF) was openly established; its members included many students and Eritrean intellectuals. In the 1970s a group of the ELF's members split and formed the Eritrean People's Liberation Front (EPLF), a Communist rebel movement. Not only did the rebels fight the Ethiopian government, but the discord created among them generated a civil war. Eventually the two Eritrean groups would combine, united by their loathing for Ethiopia.

Yohannes Mengsteab joined the EPLF in 1976, propelled by his desire for what was right for his country but as part of the Communist insurgency. As an EPLF member, he had given up his Christian faith. But on this evening, under the stars, with death a real possibility, Yohannes was brought to his knees. He couldn't help but comfort himself by thinking about his home in the Christian village of Deki-worasi, where he'd grown up.

Yohannes wished he could sit in the outdoor common area among other men and women of his village as they joked, laughed, and sang while cooking the *injera* bread. He loved sitting in the open air while the bread was cooked over an open fire on a hot plate called a *mogogo*. He thought fondly of the bright woven bags rolled down at the top to expose the spices contained within: salt, cardamom, and saffron. He remembered clay bricks resting all day as the sun baked them solid. The village men would use the dried bricks to build many things around the village, like another open-air fireplace or the base of a home.

He recalled the comfort it brought him to look at the many *hidmo*, homes made of small stones, rocks, and clay and covered with thatched roofs, clustered together in the village. Each *hidmo* was separated into two rooms: the kitchen in the rear and the public room, which also served as sleeping quarters, in the front. He thought of his home and of his brothers and sisters nudging and kicking one another aside for more sleeping space. How he wished he were there now with them instead of sharing space with soldiers, many of whom he didn't know—many of whom would be dead in the morning. The simplicity and comfort of his village would no longer look the same after the ugliness of war.

Yohannes, a boy brought up by loving Christian parents who taught him to trust in Jesus as Lord, had made a long journey to reject that upbringing.

CHAPTER 2

Childhood in Deki-worasi

UNLIKE MANY OF HIS ELF comrades, Yohannes was educated. He grew up in the Christian village of Deki-worasi, the fifth of nine children. His parents were farmers and made their living by working their farm and selling their goods to local markets. Yohannes's father had taught himself to read the Bible, and he'd gather his family together before bed to sing hymns and read daily devotions. Yohannes's parents were devoted to the Lord and their children; they were one of the few families in the village to send all of their children to school. While it would have been financially advantageous to have all nine children work on the farm, Yohannes's parents felt that a full education would best prepare their children for a twentieth-century economy—an economy where knowledge and learning would be necessary for success.

Yohannes went to a parochial Lutheran school through the fourth grade. His elementary education was reinforced through the rural congregation his family belonged to. While its members did not have a full-time pastor, lay villagers took turns evangelizing and leading worship each week. Each villager's strength of faith was more palpable than the last villager's. Yohannes grew up strong in his faith, feeling his love for Jesus grow and seeing how anyone who truly believed could live out the power of the priesthood and disseminate Christ's message. It was the passion of the simple villagers that ignited Yohannes's faith and life. For example, Yohannes's kindergarten teacher, Mr. Gehbrewoldi, a deacon in the church, was a strict but loving man. While Yohannes was a quick learner and was always motivated, discipline was a bit of a problem for him, as it is for many young children. Mr. Gehbrewoldi taught Yohannes the importance of self-discipline in a loving and Christian manner.

"Children," Mr. Gehbrewoldi would quietly command, waiting a few moments for the rowdy din created by rambunctious children to dissipate slowly. These children were used to spending full days in the outdoors, tending to the animals on their farms and singing loudly as they worked. When they were able to take a break, the children would find a soccer ball and start a pickup game on a flat patch of land. Puffs of dust, kicked up from their game, followed raucous laughter and playful shouts as the game went on. Studiousness and respectful quiet were unnatural to these children, but these qualities needed to be taught so the children could learn.

When enough eager faces turned his way, Mr. Gehbrewoldi would continue. "Idle hands are the devil's work, children. Everywhere we turn, the devil tries to tempt us. Sometimes he makes us wish we were outside playing rather than in the schoolhouse learning our lessons. But we must have enough discipline to ignore the devil. We need to take many breaks from the world around us each day to stop and listen. When we do that, we will hear Jesus, and the devil can tempt us no longer. This is called being disciplined. When we are disciplined, we are called to act like Jesus's disciples. We hear his words and act on them."

Yohannes vowed to himself that he would remain disciplined, hear Jesus's words, and never give up despite any challenges he would face.

For fifth and sixth grades, Yohannes and his siblings walked to a neighboring village for their studies. According to his teacher, Mr. Tafere, Yohannes was the best student in his classroom. Because of this he endured much bullying from his classmates. They made fun of him for always having his nose buried in a book, for reading instead of playing, for being the teacher's favorite student, and for always having the right answer. Children tend to mock what they do not understand, and this was something Yohannes knew all too well; he had experienced it often with his eight brothers and sisters.

But knowing why this was happening to him did not take away the sting and the hurt when the insults were directed at him. This teasing, however, did not deter Yohannes from his studies and from achieving good grades. In fact, when he pushed away the hurt, it only inspired him to work harder. He wanted to prove to those children who mocked him as well as to himself that he was smart, willing, and disciplined, and that he would achieve many great things in his life.

One night after he had finished studying, Yohannes's mother accidentally dropped his notebooks on the wood-burning stove, setting his notes on fire. When he saw that half of his notes were charred and unreadable, Yohannes panicked. He was using these notes to prepare himself for finals.

"Yohannes, I am so very sorry," his mother exclaimed, clutching him close to her. "I know how important this is to you," she said, her tears threatening to fall. "What can I do?" she asked, knowing money to buy new notebooks was scant. But more importantly, she knew months of notes would be nearly impossible to recover this close to final examinations. It was these very examinations that would determine whether or not Yohannes would earn acceptance into seventh grade. The guilt over her mistake overwhelmed his mother. She knew how much moving into seventh grade meant to Yohannes. It was important to her too.

"I will have to do my best with the notes I have remaining," Yohannes said, returning his mother's embrace. He was angry and afraid that without his notes he'd be unable to prepare properly for the examinations. But he forgave his mother; it was an honest mistake. Yohannes had two choices ahead of him: he could not even bother studying and blame any failure on what had happened to his notes, or he could discipline himself and continue studying the notes that remained in an effort to do his best.

When the children in his classroom saw Yohannes's half-burned and virtually useless notebooks, those who bullied him turned even crueler in their criticisms.

"Look at Yohannes's books," one of the children said loudly enough to draw the attention of several surrounding students.

"Yohannes isn't so smart after all," said another. "How dumb do you have to be to burn your notes?"

Yohannes sat quietly, waiting for Mr. Tafere to begin class. He tried his best to tune out the insults that he heard from the students who sat around him. Words like *dumb, stupid,* and *idiot* burned into him like a hot poker. Yohannes thought it would be better to be punched than to feel the pain of these words.

Mr. Tafere faced his class. He looked down at the remains of Yohannes's notebook, immediately understanding why the class was in an uproar so early in the day. "Class," he said. "I wanted to discuss with you what happened at Yohannes's house last night." Yohannes heard the snickers from some of the boys who'd been calling him names.

"It is a story of misfortune and great dedication," Mr. Tafere continued, ignoring the rude students. "You see, Yohannes is a very dedicated student. And a disciplined one. He studies every night because he wants to do well on his exams." Then Mr. Tafere did something unusual: he lied. "Last night Yohannes was up late studying by the light of an oil lamp. But he became very tired, and he fell asleep with his head on the table. The oil lamp fell over and burned half of his notes." Turning to the astounded young student, Mr. Tafere addressed Yohannes. "If only all students would be as determined as you to do so well on their exams." He looked to his class again. "You should all take a lesson from Yohannes and study as hard as him."

Knowing his teacher believed in him, even though the students in his class did not, Yohannes became more inspired. It would have been easy for Yohannes to give up and not continue to work hard. His discipline and his love for his studies motivated him even further to excel: he earned the highest score in the whole district in the national standardized testing. His score earned him a scholarship to go to a boarding school for seventh grade. The boarding school was in Asmara, a port city and the capital of Eritrea.

The boarding school Yohannes attended was run by Swedish missionaries. Yohannes attended this school from the seventh through tenth grades. He was very active in school and church throughout this time. He actively participated in Sunday school, sang in the youth choir, joined the Gospel Team to do evangelistic outreach within the village of Asmara, and distributed tracts and Bibles on the streets. In addition to his studies, Yohannes dedicated himself to absorbing the world around him, absorbing how impactful Christian outreach was. He felt great love for disseminating the word of Christ to everyone he could; if just one person would accept the word of Christ, that would be enough for him. Just making someone aware of Christ's love by handing that person a pamphlet could lead him or her to salvation. The passion to disseminate the word of Christ that had been ignited in Yohannes as a youth in the village of Deki-worasi was now further nurtured at the boarding school in Asmara.

The director at the boarding school, Mr. Stahlberg, a Swedish missionary, took a special interest in Yohannes. First, it was Yohannes's intelligence that caught Mr. Stahlberg's eye.

"Yohannes," he said, following Yohannes down the hallway one afternoon. "Have you ever played chess?"

Yohannes furrowed his brow, thinking. "No," he replied. "Not regularly, anyway. I don't know the rules."

"Would you like me to teach you?" Mr. Stahlberg asked with a smile.

"Yes," Yohannes replied excitedly. The prospect of spending time with one of his favorite teachers and learning a new game held much appeal for him. Soon Mr. Stahlberg began to invite Yohannes to play chess with him daily; in these sessions Mr. Stahlberg taught Yohannes the game and simple strategies. Yohannes soon became quite adept at the game, mastering the techniques Mr. Stahlberg had taught him and developing strategies that were all his own. The first time Yohannes beat his mentor, Yohannes couldn't help but celebrate his achievement. Many would consider his outburst unsportsmanlike, but Mr. Stahlberg looked at Yohannes's accomplishment with pride. Yohannes had always worked hard at everything he did. Mastering chess was no exception.

While working with Yohannes in class and also while playing chess with him, Mr. Stahlberg recognized the depth of spirituality that Yohannes held within, his pure passion for learning and then sharing the word of Christ. Seeing this, Mr. Stahlberg prayed with Yohannes and invited him to join in his daily devotions. Honored at this invitation, Yohannes eagerly accepted. In the boarding school's small prayer room, Yohannes spent much time reflecting—just talking to God and praying that he would remain on the path God set forth for him.

CHAPTER 3

The New Regime

IN 1974 EMPEROR HAILE SELASSIE of Ethiopia was overthrown in a coup led by a rebel faction with a Marxist-Leninist agenda. At first, the transitional government was quite unpopular in Eritrea, which was still a part of Ethiopia. The Communist government, however, did not have the financial backing to form a strong military to enforce its politics. This gave the Eritrean Liberation Movement a position of strength, allowing it to grow its numbers to put pressure on this new Ethiopian government. The Communists sought recruits especially among the young; they targeted schools and study groups to recruit young people for their movement.

Eventually the Soviet Union stepped in and supported the fledgling Ethiopian government. This support brought Soviet military strategies and Communism into the new government, which was called was called the Derg, short for "Coordinating Committee of the Armed Forces, Police, and Territorial Army" in the Ethiopian-Eritrean language Ge'ez. The Derg regime worked to gain complete control of Ethiopia, Eritrea, and Somalia by teaching Communist tenets and spreading the agenda demanded by the Soviet Union.

General Aman Mikael Andom became the acting head of state in Ethiopia after the fall of Emperor Haile Selassie. He was an Eritrean and also a Lutheran. He had been dismissed by Emperor Selassie and had been elected to serve in the Ethiopian Senate in exile.

Once Emperor Selassie was removed from power, the Derg appointed General Andom as its chairman. But then a strange thing happened: General Andom became at odds with the Derg, in particular with Mengistu Haile Mariam, another of the Derg leaders. General Andom didn't feel the execution of the Ethiopian aristocrats and former Ethiopian government officials who'd served under Emperor Selassie was necessary. Rather, he found that approach cruel and barbaric. As an Ethiopian he wanted to create a peaceful settlement with the Eritrean Liberation Front rather than attempt to gain control by force.

Andom made two personal visits to Eritrea, during which he gave speeches to villagers and ELF members alike promising that with the end of the imperial regime would come a government that would unify the two nations; this new government, Andom claimed, would restore peace and prosperity to Eritrea and Ethiopia. General Andom also promised that he would investigate the war crimes and human rights violations the Ethiopians carried out against the Eritreans and that he would punish the guilty. This excited the ELF, and its members put their trust and faith in General Andom, praying that he'd be able to fulfill his promises. After so many years of war, a peaceful settlement would be more than welcome.

In the end, though, the Derg overruled General Andom's ideas and began eliminating any opposition within its military ranks. Derg members attacked the Imperial Bodyguard, the air force, and the Corps of Engineers because the Derg had become aware that there was resistance to the new government among these groups. General Andom's hopes that no blood would be shed were squelched.

General Andom sought support in protest of the Derg in hopes of reining it in. Andom looked to the army and the rest of the common people for support. He sent communication to all military units, highly criticizing the Derg and its approach to ruling the country. Meanwhile, Mengistu Haile Mariam demanded the Derg send five thousand men to Eritrea to contain the ELF movement by whatever measures were necessary. General Andom refused to carry out those orders and resigned his government post. Andom secretly sent appeals to his supporters, but Mengistu Haile Mariam intercepted the general's appeals. General Andom died in a battle with the military personnel sent to arrest him. With his death and with the Communist Party now infiltrating Somalia, the Eritreans lost hope and knew they'd have to work alone to secure their independence.

One bloody night in January 1975, a battle between the Eritrean Liberation Movement and the Ethiopians broke out in the city of Asmara, where Yohannes was attending boarding school. All hell broke loose as Ethiopian forces moved in, randomly executing young Eritreans and throwing their bodies into the streets. The panicked city ceased all activities, and the public officials urged everyone to remain indoors. But despite all warnings, the Ethiopians became increasingly more hostile, and Asmara became more dangerous with each passing hour, especially for a young male. Ethiopian forces aggressively continued their foray within the city, targeting the young men in particular. Bodies of male students began piling up; their blood ran through the streets.

The whole city was a battle zone. The cracks and pops of gunfire raged on all sides. The electricity was out, food was in short supply, and the water supply had been shut off. The citizens of Asmara had to depend on one another for security, obtaining the limited goods that were available, and sheer survival. Civilian casualties continued to mount. One source estimated that nearly one thousand were dead and another thousand were wounded during this siege. The United Nations granted the Red Cross permission to provide food rations to Asmara.

Yohannes and his cousin, Abrahaley Sium, who was also attending school in Asmara, felt they had no recourse but to run for their lives. So far they'd been lucky; they had remained in the city through two weeks of the conflict, depending on the kindness of strangers for food and shelter. They tried to remain as inconspicuous as possible because the Ethiopian forces were targeting young men their age in the ongoing slaughter. Trying to leave through the main roads of the city would be dangerous, even suicidal. Yohannes and Abrahaley found as much food as they could carry easily and decided to make their way cautiously to the eastern side of the city. From there they planned to walk around the mountains toward their home in Deki-worasi, a little less than sixty miles from Asmara.

It seemed like an eternity before they got to a region known as Tsilima. They arrived around dusk on their first day of travel. They came upon a dwelling, where they begged the family to allow them to stay for the night. Thank God, knowing they had traveled from Asmara and had fled the ongoing battle, the family was welcoming and willing to accommodate Yohannes and his cousin. The two young men awoke early the next morning and finished the nearly twenty-four-hour journey to their village.

Yohannes's mother and father swept him up in their arms, tears streaming down their faces. Other family members and friends gave thanks and praise to the Lord that Yohannes and Abrahaley had returned to them unharmed. While Yohannes was equally as grateful that he and his cousin had been spared, he could not overcome the horrors of what he'd experienced. Because of the carnage and the blatant disrespect for life the Ethiopian military had shown the Eritreans, Yohannes was now a firm believer in Eritrea's need for independence, and he put his whole heart into joining the Eritrean Liberation Front.

CHAPTER 4

Jesus Said, "You Will Deny Me Three Times"

YOHANNES MENGSTEAB WAS EAGER TO fight to defend his country. He had been indoctrinated by the ELF cadres and had become a willing part of the political movement. He believed that true peace and security for Eritrea could only come through the barrel of a gun. After five years of working closely with the ELF he was preparing to do just that—but his Christian faith was now a burden.

He repressed his faith in order to serve the ELF rather than trying to nurture his faith and reconcile it with the notion of war. Deference to the war at hand, rather than developing his faith and finding a better solution than war, was the trick Satan played on Yohannes during this period in his life. A form of complacency settled within Yohannes, as he believed this surrender to Eritrean politics might really be his destiny. Yohannes's belief in independence for Eritrea blurred the lines between right and wrong with which he had grown up.

The young man received only three months of basic training and three months of additional training from the Iraqi military before he was told he was prepared to fight. The only weaponry the ELF had was what it had gathered after past battles with the Ethiopians.

By 1977 the ELF was prepared to push the Ethiopians from Eritrea by working with Somalia to simultaneously invade Ethiopia and thus drain Ethiopia's resources. But because of an influx of arms to Ethiopia from the Soviet Union, the Derg defeated the Somalians and forced the ELF to retreat and rethink its strategy.

Now, in 1978, after a brief respite from war, Yohannes had been called up to fight against the Ethiopians, who were backed by the Soviet Union and Cuba. He heard the call and came willingly, but his willingness did not come without reservations.

As he prepared for his first battle, he tried to sleep on the hard earth, with rocks and rubble digging into his shoulders and back. But he hardly felt these small annoyances; his thoughts wandered far away. As hard as he tried, although he knew he was to risk his life tomorrow for a formidable cause close to his heart, he was still unable to find peace. He counted down the moments until the battle while staring at the stars and listening to the cattle baying in the distance; he waited for the fighting to begin and his fate, of life or death, to be revealed.

"My friend," Yohannes's comrade to the left whispered. In the utter silence, his voice sounded as loud as a mortar round raining in. Yohannes turned his head toward him. "I can't wait to see the Ethiopians' faces when they see their own tanks chasing them." Unable to help himself, Yohannes felt a laugh swell from deep within his belly. Just in time he managed to stifle it to a soft chuckle so as not to draw attention from the others. Much of the weaponry the Eritreans would use in this assault was taken from previous encounters with the Ethiopians.

"Thank you," Yohannes said, "I needed that laugh." His comrade laughed quietly beside him. Yohannes found himself a bit more at ease and fell into a light sleep.

The battle began just before dawn on July 14, 1975.

Artillery shells exploded around their camp in thunderous blasts. Acacia trees shook with outgoing mortar fire that sounded like the rhythmic turning of the blades of a helicopter, only much louder. Small arms fire cracked all about, like a toddler stomping on a sheet of bubble wrap; spent shells dropped into the sand, and puffs of dust rose around them. Yohannes looked to his comrade next to him, the one who had made the jokes he had found so humorous. He saw the sweat run down his friend's face, his lips pulled back in a sneer to reveal his teeth clenched together, the muscle in his jaw bouncing each time he pulled the trigger.

Yohannes looked through the sight of his own gun. He willed his hands to stop shaking and focus. His finger found the trigger, which felt unusually cool in the sweltering Eritrean heat. It was still hot outside now, even though the sun had yet to rise, and it would only get hotter. The acidic smell of gunpowder surrounded him, the thickness of it inescapable. Yohannes felt the sweat collecting on his brow, and he pulled the trigger. He kept shooting at his enemy, the rival preventing his country from its independence, from any opportunity. He kept shooting for everybody he'd seen lying on the streets of Asmara, for every young life that had been taken for naught. He kept shooting for his brothers and sisters at home, whose opportunities for a better life would be taken away by the Ethiopians. He kept shooting. This moment, this battle, would forever change him.

A mortar round crashed right in front of their camp. The world went silent for a moment; a high-pitched beep, like one of the high-frequency tones on a hearing test, rang through Yohannes's ears. Instantaneous pain tore through his ankle. The world went dark for a moment, and Yohannes nearly passed out from the agony of it. He dropped his gun and grabbed at his leg, knowing it was bad before even looking at the wound. He turned to his comrade to tell him he needed to retreat, that he needed help.

Tears filled Yohannes's eyes. He now saw that his comrade had taken the majority of the force of the mortar round and was dead. His blank eyes looked back at Yohannes, registering nothing, their light and laughter forever gone. Yohannes cried out, his heart heavy with the ache of war and with sorrow for his fallen comrade.

"Lord," Yohannes prayed, "if You allow this kind of pain and ugliness into the world, You must not exist at all." His heart grew cold, and then everything went black.

Yohannes was unable to return to battle after that day. His ankle had been severely injured, and he could no longer run and be useful on the front lines. He was sent home.

Back in his village, he joined the Good Samaritan Department and helped distribute vaccinations and assist farmers who needed a hand. Yohannes led a quieter life after his days of battle, going through the motions, helping out where he could, his life an easy, comfortable state of affairs. He kept the trauma he'd felt after the battle hidden away in a locked room in his brain so he didn't have to face it. He did the same with his faith.

In 1979 the two competing Eritrean liberation factions, the ELF and the EPLF, fought each other for control of Eritrea. The ELF was pushed out of Eritrea into the Sudan. Yohannes, since he had been aligned with the ELF, was now forced to flee—he ended up in an ELF camp in the Sudan along with his fellow comrades.

As he spent his days and nights living in this camp, with much time to reflect, Yohannes turned back to God. "You saved me, Lord," Yohannes remembered. "You answered my prayers even though I didn't realize it at the time. I asked You to save my life during that battle, and You did. And my repayment was to denounce You, not serve You. I've sinned, and I beg for Your forgiveness."

He reexamined the notion of Communism, and to him it now seemed so foolish. He recalled the faith he and his family shared when he was a child: his father reading them devotions; the small but mighty congregation he worshipped with in his village; and the circles the children would form, singing and telling Bible stories. And then Yohannes realized that it was God who was prodding him to continue the journey He had set forth for him, guiding him along a path already prepared for him, and that God was still ready to speak when Yohannes was ready to listen. Yohannes rejoiced at knowing that God was once again working through him, His imperfect but willing vessel.

CHAPTER 5

The Return of the
Prodigal Son

YOHANNES DECIDED TO LEAVE THE ELF camp in response to his desire
to satisfy a growing need to continue upon the spiritual journey opening
quickly before him. He and a friend, Kiflay Habte, knew of a refugee
camp in the Sudan in Kassala, a bordering city between Eritrea and the
Sudan. Swedish Christian missionaries served there; this seemed like a
good fit to Yohannes because Swedish missionaries were the ones who
had planted the roots of Christianity in his village. He knew if he could
get to Kassala, he would be renewed in his faith.

In the mid-nineteenth century, Swedish Lutheran missionaries had
come to Africa with the goal of spreading the word of Christ and doing
the Lord's work in Ethiopia. As they moved closer to the Ethiopian border with Eritrea, there was a tribal war among some of the Ethiopians.
With no other recourse, the missionaries had to move back toward the
Red Sea. They met up with a faction of Coptic priests and formed a
small church in Eritrea. The Christian faith bloomed within Eritrea as
a result of the efforts of the Swedish and Coptic priests working together. The rich history of Lutherans in Eritrea, combined with Yohannes's
own parochial education, made the desire to reconnect to his roots all
the more paramount.

Yohannes and Kiflay left the ELF camp on foot in the early evening and arrived at the outskirts of Kassala in the middle of the night. They found a safe spot in which to huddle together to spend the rest of the night. They would look for food and shelter in the morning.

"What do you hope to accomplish here, Yohannes?" His friend was always curious about Yohannes's motivation.

"I need to reconnect with the Swedish missionaries serving this camp," Yohannes replied. "When I joined the ELF, I let the spiritual side of me slip away. I didn't realize until I was in the ELF camp how foolish that was."

"Yohannes, do not even think about becoming a pastor," Kiflay said with a laugh.

Yohannes joined in, his roaring laugh coming easily. "Me? A pastor? No way!" he exclaimed, and both young men shook with laughter.

The young men sought shelter and food the next day. A kind family opened their home to them and offered a bed to sleep on and food to eat. About a week later, Yohannes connected with Lutheran pastor Tuquabo Teclegiorgis, who was serving Eritrean refugees, like himself, in Kassala. Upon meeting Yohannes, Tuquabo Teclegiorgis sensed this young Eritrean's strength of faith.

"Yohannes," he called. Yohannes looked up from the book he was reading and, with a smile, walked over to the pastor.

"Pastor Teclegiorgis, how can I help you today?" Yohannes asked eagerly, willing to accept any assignment the pastor was willing to entrust him with.

"Would you like to serve as an evangelist here at camp?" Pastor Teclegiorgis asked. "You have strong faith, and those here would benefit from your preaching."

Yohannes was astounded, but he didn't hesitate before accepting the pastor's offer. Though he was a layman and would be acting as an itinerant preacher, Yohannes saw the clear opportunity to share his faith, and through that sharing he could strengthen his own. Yohannes knew that through accepting this position, he'd never regret his return to the Lord's plan for his life; he understood that finally he was moving along the path the Lord had intended for him. He smiled to himself as he remembered his disbelief that he would ever become a pastor.

Yohannes began preaching, leading prayer, and sharing the words of Christ with all who would listen to him. He preached whenever he had the chance, and the refugees in camp with him listened. Yohannes's heart swelled with joy, and his passion was rekindled. What had been but a flickering flame lost within him was now an open fire, burning through him.

In the fall of 1981, Yohannes moved from the Kassala camp to the city of Gedaref, located near a cluster of refugee camps. There Yohannes became involved with other Swedish missionaries, clergy who headed the Sudanese Council of Churches' Eastern Relief Program. He was made the interpreter for its director, Reverend Bertil Holmgren. While servicing the camps near Gedaref, Yohannes shared the leadership of the morning devotions for the staff. He also led a small Bible study group in the city and organized a children's ministry in one of the refugee camps. Being with the children reminded him of his days as a child in his village, where he joyfully sang and played soccer with his friends.

Reverend Holmgren valued Yohannes; he enjoyed his sense of humor, his drive, and his spirituality. When he recognized how devout Yohannes was and how his preaching affected everyone who listened in such a positive way, he asked Yohannes a most important question.

"Yohannes, I think it's time you are catechized. I'd be honored to have the opportunity to be the one to do so," Reverend Holmgren said.

Overwhelmed at the process, Yohannes quickly agreed. He'd been spiritually starved for the five long years he served in the ELF and had been indoctrinated into their socialist and Communist ways. His duty to evangelize had elevated his spirituality to some degree, and he could have been satisfied with that for a long time. But the opportunity to be catechized took the fire of passion that burned in his chest and stoked it even higher.

Reverend Holmgren used the 1986 Concordia Publishing House edition of Luther's *Small Catechism with Explanation* for Yohannes's catechism class. He challenged Yohannes to memorize it. Once Yohannes had memorized the book, drinking it down like a man who'd thirsted for days, Reverend Holmgren challenged Yohannes again. He gave him opportunities to lead devotions for the office staff and to start an outreach program within the refugee camp. Yohannes relished the trust he was given. Committed to his service, Yohannes took in each task with the innocent abandon of a child finally able to run for the first time. Reverend Holmgren then challenged Yohannes to consider going into full-time ministry. Yohannes knew God had forgiven him for defying Him and denouncing his faith, but now the Lord had put a challenge in front of him to test the true strength of his faith.

Yohannes had not considered full-time ministry up to this point. In fact, he had scoffed at it. But here was God, through Reverend Holmgren, asking Yohannes to serve Him. He understood this decision would mean a true return to the home of his Father. Yohannes had been the prodigal son, but now he was returning to his Father's house and was being welcomed to serve Him. This was a true spiritual rebirth that changed the entire trajectory of the prodigal's life.

CHAPTER 6

New Life in New York

IN 1982 ERITREAN REFUGEES WERE offered the opportunity for resettlement in the United States and other nations through the United Nations Commission for Refugees program. While he enjoyed working for the Sudan Council of Churches' Eastern Relief Program, Yohannes knew there was more waiting for him elsewhere. It would have been easy for him to stay in Gedaref, working comfortably and safely as an interpreter for Reverend Holmgren. He could still preach on occasion, minister, and evangelize. He had developed the children's ministry program and Bible study; certainly there were other things he could do while working there. But Yohannes wanted something more and knew he could serve the Lord in a different way. He had applied to a Lutheran seminary in the Sudan but was turned away. He was determined to find a way to become a pastor.

Feeling he could acquire no more knowledge where he was, he decided the best chance he had to be ordained was to go to the United States—an impossible dream. The United States was accepting refugees from the Sudan, but not many. He applied anyway.

After a multitude of interviews serving to measure the potential for successful acclimation to a new country, Yohannes was accepted into the resettlement program. However, he delayed coming to the United States until he completed his high school education equivalency

requirements. He did this the hard way, through correspondence courses from Cambridge College in England. Yohannes knew that coming
to America with as much education as he could acquire would only
serve to help achieve acceptance into a seminary. The now former
Communist soldier took his high school equivalency final exam in the
city of Khartoum in May 1983. He set foot on the ground in the United
States on June 23, 1983. What relief! What joy! How frightening.

Yohannes had a glimpse of the United States through movies and
books, and this exposure helped to cultivate his expectations. Part of his
preparation for resettlement had included cultural orientation—but the
preparations he'd received paled in comparison to what Yohannes encountered once he walked onto the streets of New York City. Jokingly,
Yohannes said that arriving in New York City would be a "new culture
even for a midwesterner," and it certainly was culture shock for an immigrant with a poor grasp of English.

The Hebrew Immigrant Aid Society (HIAS) had sponsored
Yohannes's trip to the United States. He and several other refugees were
flown from Khartoum to Athens. They stayed in Athens overnight
and then took a direct flight to New York City. There were approxi-
mately fifty refugees on the plane to the United States, and Yohannes
was the only refugee on the plane slated to remain in New York. The
others were being dispersed throughout the country to their sponsoring agencies. When the plane landed at Kennedy Airport, he gathered
his few belongings and was escorted via taxi to a hotel near the Macy's
building. The taxi driver handed Yohannes a map of the city and told
him which building to go to in order to check into the hotel. At this
point, HIAS's partnering agency, the New York Association for New
Americans (NYANA), took over Yohannes's case.

Thank God for NYANA. It was originally founded in 1949 to assist Holocaust refugees who were arriving in the United States. In 1972
NYANA began serving non-Jewish refugees, including those from

Africa, Cambodia, and Tibet. NYANA strove to provide one-stop services to refugees. These services included assistance finding housing, health and family services, a school to learn English, vocational assistance and training, and courses to help the immigrants adjust to their new country.

For the first couple of weeks, Yohannes felt lonely and often overwhelmed. His English was sketchy; he had only a few words here and there. He'd walk down lengths of crowded pavement with people rushing by, their heads down, few making eye contact with him. It appeared as if the people living and working in the city were propelled by a special type of sonar; they were somehow able to skirt around unmoving people and objects without looking up. Yohannes, desperate for someone to take notice of him and to offer to help him, quickly became intimidated by his new surroundings. Had he been in Eritrea, he simply would have had to ask for help and someone would come to his aid. In the United States, however, it was not so simple. He learned he would need to assert himself here in order to be successful. He came to understand that the inhabitants of New York City weren't purposely ignoring him; rather, it was simply a product of the culture and the pace of the city. The inhabitants had no time to spare for anything or anyone else other than their own agendas. New York was completely different from any African city he'd visited, even the most populated.

During these first few weeks, Yohannes barely left his hotel room. He'd walk from his room to the elevators, travel to the ground floor, and then walk to the local pizza shop about a block away. He ate lots and lots of pizza; it was cheap, the restaurant was close by, and American pizza was like nothing he'd ever eaten before. Yet, it reminded him of home, of the Italian restaurants that still existed in Eritrea after the Italian army left. The pizza in New York was delicious.

Often Yohannes would search the night sky while chewing his pizza, looking for the bright stars that had often comforted him at home in

Eritrea, those stars that spelled out Christ's message for him. It was hard to see those stars here in New York City; they were faint and blurred. Christ's words, often difficult for Yohannes to decipher even under the clearest night sky, were impossible to discern here. He struggled to read what these stars were telling him. Was the fact that they were so difficult to read meant to give Yohannes a foreboding message or just to tell him that his path wasn't yet clear? Or was there a deeper message he had yet to discover while here in the United States?

Struggling to make sense of his new surroundings, his purpose, and how his spirituality could be nurtured during this transitional period in the United States, Yohannes discovered an Episcopalian church in Manhattan very close to his hotel. He walked into the church and chose a pew in which to sit and pray. Much like on the street, no one chose to reach out to the African refugee. No one went out of his or her way to welcome an unfamiliar face. When he left, no one even noticed. Yohannes became further withdrawn. His effort to find a church, somewhere welcoming to all, somewhere he could be comfortable, earned him nothing positive. Yohannes became ever more worried that this resettlement had been a mistake.

CHAPTER 7

The Story behind the Face

AFTER TWO WEEKS OF INITIATION and training from the New York Association for New Americans, Yohannes was moved from his lonely hotel room into a small apartment in Brooklyn that he'd share with another refugee from Eritrea. Finally, someone he could communicate with! Someone with whom he could share his struggles and his concerns! Someone who shared his culture! Yohannes and his roommate bonded quickly, often through their food. They found ingredients common to the meals they'd had at home and began cooking Ethiopian and Eritrean dishes: *wat* (a stew) with whatever meats and vegetables that were inexpensive; *injera* bread to sop up the *wat*; and sometimes *azifa*, a green lentil salad.

Through his resettlement program, Yohannes was entitled to receive a stipend toward his apartment costs plus three months of state aid, including Medicaid and food stamps, while he worked with his sponsoring agency to find a job. Within a month Yohannes was hired at a plastics factory in Queens. It was a solitary job on an assembly line, so the language barrier he had with other employees was easily concealed. He would take the subway to his job every day, work his shift alone, and return to his apartment. Each day was the same routine—repetitive, undemanding, and simple.

Sometimes Yohannes would tire of the routine and would take his roommate with him to Central Park to have some fun. During one visit Yohannes met a gentleman named William Campbell. William's mother was from Eritrea, and his wife was Ethiopian. While William had been in the military, he was stationed at a base in Ethiopia. It was there where he met his wife. They quickly married and moved to New Jersey. William was no longer in the service, but was a delivery driver. He and his wife would sometimes spend pleasant afternoons in Central Park. Yohannes was grateful to have met a new friend, especially one who had some connection to his home country. He felt this was a sign from the Lord that things would begin to look up for him. But he had to move beyond the rigorous routine he'd developed so easily in such a brief period of time.

Yohannes wasn't at all content being stuck in a mind-numbing routine. He felt how easy it could be to become automated, like so many of the people he encountered on the subway on his way to work or in the streets around Times Square. He was becoming one of them, moving by habit through his day. His spirituality had once again been forced down within him. He had no one to speak to about Christ and no one to evangelize. He had nowhere to go for his soul's nourishment. The day came when Yohannes was determined to find somewhere he could go, a congregation where, if he had to, he would welcome himself—a place that could become his spiritual home. Determined to find the right place, Yohannes took to the streets of Times Square, this time walking with his head up, ready for a church to catch his eye.

Saint Luke's Lutheran Church on West Forty-Sixth Street caught Yohannes's eye and took his breath away. Saint Luke's is a historical church, founded in 1850 as a Dutch Reformed congregation, with its first meeting held in rented rooms on Thirty-Fifth Street. This church moved several times and finally found its forever home in its current location, where the cornerstone was laid in 1922. With its beautiful white-brick facade and spires, the church provided the refugee from Eritrea with a welcomed feeling of purity and true faith. The church gave a warmth to the concrete heart of New York City. The beauty of the church windows, in addition to the striking design of the building, has been described by David Dunlap, the *New York Times* Metro reporter, as paraphrased in Wikipedia, "a happy marriage between the Gothic Revival and Art Deco styles." To Yohannes the windows appeared as the eyes of a God who was looking down on him with love.

Yohannes entered the church and knelt in the closest pew. The grandeur of the altar inspired him to one day preach from one as beautiful as this one. Light shone through the stained glass windows, lighting the pews with colorful shapes like a kaleidoscope. Yohannes knew this was the place where he belonged.

In those days, the early 1980s, Dale Hanson was the pastor of Saint Luke's. He not only welcomed Yohannes into his congregation, but he welcomed Yohannes into his home and heart. Pastor Hanson relished inviting newer members of his congregation to his apartment in the parish house near the church. He'd never married, so he would cook dinner after Sunday fellowship services and entertain his guests with lively conversation and spiritual dialogue.

Dale would place the food on his modest kitchen table, ask everyone to sit in his or her respective seat, and open dinner with a prayer of thanksgiving. Dale had a very kind face. He had lines drawn around the corners of his mouth, smile lines, rather than frown lines crossing his forehead. His hair was still mostly blond, and he was a tall, well-fed fellow. Like the church building, Dale was full of light and compassion.

At first, Yohannes was quiet, taking in everything around him and not confident enough in his English to participate in the ongoing conversation. He'd sit listening, eating, and enjoying the meat and potatoes Pastor Hanson served his guests. Soon Yohannes became comfortable enough to discuss with Pastor Hanson what he felt his personal mission was: that he was destined to go to college and from there to the semi-nary. He told Pastor Hanson of his struggles to adapt to New York City and his troubles with the Episcopal church he'd attempted to become a part of.

Pastor Hanson put his hand on Yohannes's shoulder. "I'm sorry you've had such a troubled past, my friend. Looking at you, no one would know what it took for you to come here," he said.

"There's always a story behind the face. You just have to ask," Yohannes replied. "I may be different from other immigrants to this country, because I am working very hard to be successful. But my aware-ness has been raised to the struggles of most immigrants who are too intimidated and scared to venture out and overcome their challenges. I think my journey will involve helping new immigrants and refugees, especially Eritrean refugees."

"I think this is a noble and necessary vocation, Yohannes, and I will do whatever I can to help you."

CHAPTER 8

College Boy

YOHANNES'S JOURNEY TO CONCORDIA COLLEGE in Bronxville began with Pastor Dale Hanson's call to the Concordia admissions counselor. Before he knew it, Yohannes was enrolled in school. He applied for and received Pell and state grants, which helped him to pay for his schooling, along with student loans. He also received a small scholarship from his village in Eritrea. While going to school, Yohannes worked many hours. He worked at a gas station, a grocery store, a liquor store, and on campus at the computer lab. He also cleaned houses and worked as a night guard at the nearby IBM plant to further supplement his income and to keep his debt to a minimum.

He entered Concordia College in Bronxville as a double major in Judeo-Christian heritage studies and math. At age twenty-three he was a bit older than the other twelve pre-seminary students, and he took on the role of "older brother" with pride. He provided a supportive presence to the other students. He was a proactive and engaged student, seeking out others to befriend. Those he did befriend helped Yohannes adjust culturally, and he in turn provided them with unwavering loyalty and support.

Many of his Eritrean family and his friends tried to convince Yohannes that due to his negative experience with the governments in Eritrea, he should move into politics. He could help governments with differing views find peaceful solutions to conflict. But the professors Yohannes had the pleasure of getting to know encouraged him to stay on course and continue on his path toward the seminary. Yohannes was still struggling with English, so Professor Dean Green stepped in. He thought if Yohannes became more confident in the language, his ministry could extend beyond helping Eritrean refugees. Professor Green spent much time helping Yohannes correct his pronunciation so that he could enunciate English words correctly. It did often embarrass Yohannes when Professor Green made corrections to Yohannes's speech in public, but he knew the kindly man meant well, and this extra help did serve to help him become more comfortable with the language.

Although people on campus were kind to Yohannes, they often seemed concerned that he didn't understand some things due to differences in their cultures. To be frank, they could be very naive about Africans and the sophistication of African culture. One of the coeds had a stereo in her room, so a small group of students pretended that they wanted to show it to Yohannes, implying he'd never seen one before. Yohannes's friends Andrew and Keith (who are both now pastors) and a girl from down the hall joined Yohannes in the room of the coed who had the stereo. They encouraged the girl with the stereo to teach Yohannes how to turn it on.

When she did, Yohannes gasped, clutched his hands to his chest, and cried, "This must be the devil!"

"No, Yohannes, it's the radio," the girl with the stereo said, trying to calm Yohannes down. Then everyone, including Yohannes, began to laugh. Their joke had worked; Yohannes's college experience had become very typical of that of the average young American, filled with laughter and growing friendships.

CHAPTER 9

The Brightest Star
in the Night Sky

YOHANNES GRADUATED FROM CONCORDIA COLLEGE in Bronxville in the spring of 1987. He began preparing for the seminary, but it was at that time that the Communist influence in Ethiopia was at its height. Some of Yohannes's siblings and their families were in Ethiopia at the time, and they needed to get out. Their lives were in danger. In August 1987 Yohannes went to the Sudan in an effort to find a way to get them to safety. This was his priority now, despite his pending enrollment in the seminary.

Yohannes could not make the journey himself; it was too dangerous. He scraped together the necessary funds and paid for someone to smuggle his family from Ethiopia to where he was waiting in Khartoum. It took almost three months to get his family members out of Ethiopia and into the Sudan.

While in Khartoum, Yohannes was a guest at the home of Reverend Tuquabo Teclegiorgis, the Lutheran pastor from Kassala who had helped steer Yohannes on his life's current path. Yohannes eagerly awaited news of the safe passage of his family, but he also enjoyed being in a familiar place. The United States was bountiful; anything you wanted you could acquire fairly simply, be it goods or services. Great opportunity was available for everyone should he or she choose to work for it. It seemed as if the harder one worked in America, the more one could achieve or acquire. And in the 1980s, many people in the United States were motivated by the acquisition of "stuff": cars, radios, televisions, the latest gadgets, the fanciest clothes, the best food, and so on.

Yohannes had the blessing of growing up in a happy and faithful home in the Eritrea of the 1970s, even though his family had little beyond basic necessities. Yohannes now found the American notion of acquiring happiness through material things preposterous—yet he could understand the temptation. With this temptation the devil had a playground in which he could easily lure people away from God and toward the sinfulness of greed. Coming back to the Sudan and seeing the simplicity of everyday life there helped Yohannes remember his struggles and keep the temptation of the material things in perspective before returning to the United States.

One evening while he and Pastor Teclegiorgis were finishing dinner, they had a conversation about something that had been weighing on Yohannes's mind for a while: his desire to find a wife.

"Yohannes," said Pastor Teclegiorgis as he sopped up the remaining *wat* in his bowl with a hearty piece of *injera*. "You're eligible and almost thirty…"

"I'm not thirty yet. Don't rush me," Yohannes said, and laughed, the pastor joining in.

"Have you considered marriage?" asked Pastor Teclegiorgis, pushing his empty bowl away and leaning back in his chair, belly full. "It's been quite the topic of conversation between some of your friends and me."

Yohannes laughed. "That doesn't surprise me," he said, his wide grin failing to hide that getting married had been on his mind as well. "I've been thinking a lot about it," he admitted.

"You don't say…" joked Pastor Teclegiorgis, a twinkle in his eye.

"But it's complicated," said Yohannes. "I can't marry a woman from America. My parents are aging; it would be difficult for them to form a relationship with her. She wouldn't understand our customs or our language. And at their age, my parents would have trouble trying to understand hers. I would want my wife and family to be able to form an instant bond and to be able to communicate easily. That's important to me and to my parents."

"That's understandable, Yohannes," said the pastor.

"I've always prayed the Lord would send me a faithful Eritrean Christian woman I could marry," Yohannes continued. "That would make my parents happy. But she'd need to be willing to move to the United States. If you can find me a woman like that, Pastor, I'd love to meet her!"

Pastor Teclegiorgis grinned.

On a Sunday afternoon several weeks later, two young ladies visited the pastor's home while Yohannes was there. One of the two women immediately caught Yohannes's eye. She seemed to him the most beautiful woman he'd ever seen. She wore a sparsely adorned ankle-length white dress, common attire for Christian women in Eritrea. The simplicity of the traditional dress made her all the more beautiful.

Pastor Teclegiorgis welcomed the two women into his home, and the four of them shared a meal and began conversing. During this conversation Yohannes learned that the two women were cousins and the woman he was enamored with was named Alemash. Yohannes also learned that her extended family were faithful members of the Eritrean Evangelical Lutheran Church and that he knew some of them. Coincidentally, Yohannes's mother and Alemash's mother had grown up together in the same village. With so much history among their families already, Yohannes's interest in Alemash grew even more.

Yohannes and Alemash decided to take a walk outside in the evening. He wanted to once again look upon the bright stars that shone in the Eritrean night sky.

"I know that wherever you are in the world, you look upon the same stars each night," Yohannes said, "but the stars don't look the same in America. They're blurry and faded there."

"Why do you think that is?" Alemash asked.

"I always thought the stars were the Lord's words. Everyone could look upon them and find the words he or she needed to be inspired. Maybe the people in America are no longer inspired. Maybe their spirits are blurry; maybe they've lost their way," Yohannes said. "I know I am there for a reason. I know I am there to help, but I sometimes wonder how I can. I know the Lord has a plan for me—I just wish he'd tell me what it is."

"Maybe the stars aren't the Lords words, Yohannes," Alemash said softly. "Maybe each one represents someone the Lord has chosen to speak and teach His words. Here in the Sudan, in Eritrea, we are blessed to have so many messengers. That is why the stars are so bright. Missionaries from all over the world come to us to teach us about Christ. In New York City, maybe there are less people who are listening to Christ's words through his messengers. That could be why the light of their stars isn't as bright."

Yohannes and Alemash quickly decided to get married. As was customary, the future husband had to have the potential union blessed. Alemash's uncle, Berhe Habgu, blessed the union, and the beautiful couple married in the Sudan.

The handful of months Yohannes spent in Khartoum had been life-altering. He'd ensured the safety of four of his siblings, his sister-in-law, and his nephew, and he'd gotten married to a woman he fell in love with at first sight. Again, Yohannes saw that he was faced with a great choice. He could follow the Lord's path and return to the United States, leaving his wife behind until she could join him later. Doing this he could attend the seminary as he'd planned, finally being called to help Eritrean refugees resettle in America. Or he could return to

America and follow what he saw as the devil's path, the path of complacency—that choice of comfort and routine, that flowering tendril that he understood stemmed from the sin of gluttony and that required little hard work and no sacrifice. Yohannes's third and final choice would be to remain in the Sudan with his family, his wife, and so many of his friends so that he could minister to the Eritreans in the refugee camps alongside Pastor Teclegiorgis.

"Alemash, I am at a crossroads with this decision," Yohannes said, confiding in his wife. "I don't want to leave you."

"I will miss you, Yohannes. You must know that," Alemash told him, wrapping her arms around her husband in a gentle embrace. "But those people in America need you. I remember when you told me their stars don't shine as bright there. They need someone to help them. And when they look up to pray, they will finally see one bright star that stands out from the rest. That star, Yohannes, is you. You will be the one to bring so many people hope and peace. For them, you must go and finish your studies."

CHAPTER 10

The Call

IN NOVEMBER 1987 YOHANNES MENGSTEAB made his way to Saint Louis and began studying at the Saint Louis Concordia Seminary. There he reconnected with many of his friends from Concordia College Bronxville who had been pre-seminary students alongside him. Although he had left his wife and family behind, he had a homecoming of sorts when he returned to the seminary.

Yohannes had to work extremely hard while studying at the Saint Louis seminary. His studies were challenging and took a lot of his time and effort, plus he still had to find time to work to support both his new wife and his family members back in the Sudan while also paying his bills and student loans.

After living his first semester on campus at the seminary, Yohannes knew he had to start preparing for the eventual arrival of his wife. He decided to move from the beautiful campus in Clayton, a suburb of Saint Louis, into an Eritrean and Ethiopian area nearby. He moved into an apartment under Section 8, a program managed by the US Department of Housing and Urban Development that provides financial assistance to low-income individuals and families. He found this apartment with help from people in the Eritrean and Ethiopian community whom Yohannes had befriended. Yohannes was pleased with his home and was proud to have Alemash join him as soon as possible.

Just before he received his vicarage assignment (in the Lutheran Church a vicar is a third-year seminarian intern), Yohannes got word that at last his wife would be able to join him in the United States. It had been two long years since he had last seen her before becoming a student at Concordia. On March 30, 1989, Yohannes rushed to the airport as quickly as he could in the ten inches of snow that had fallen that day. On his way to the airport, he stopped and purchased a winter coat for Alemash, knowing she wouldn't have brought anything like that with her from the Sudan. He greeted her with a huge embrace and a warm coat.

Several months later, in July 1989, Yohannes and Alemash uprooted themselves from their comfortable apartment in Saint Louis to move to East Moline, Illinois, for Yohannes's vicarage assignment. Yohannes would work at Saint John's Lutheran Church in East Moline, about 160 miles northwest of Springfield, Illinois. It is a small, quiet town with a population of just under twenty-two thousand people, a stark contrast to the bustle of Saint Louis and certainly to the constant surge of New York.

Dick Behnke was the vicarage supervisor at Saint John's Lutheran Church, and he welcomed Yohannes and Alemash with open arms. Alemash didn't speak any English, so Reverend Behnke's mother-in-law, Viola, took great care to help Alemash acclimate to parish life.

Yohannes was quickly accepted by this wonderful congregation. His wit and his dedication to the Bible study program that he was helping with allowed people of the parish to enjoy Yohannes's presence. They welcomed his contributions to their parish. Soon Alemash and Yohannes were expecting their first child. In January 1990 their first son, Samson, was born. How the congregation celebrated his birth!

In 1991 Yohannes's vicarage assignment was over, and he, Alemash, and their beautiful young son returned to the Saint Louis Concordia Seminary. For convenience they moved into seminary housing. Shortly thereafter, their second son was born, and they named him Paulus. Yohannes and his family felt fully embraced by the seminary community. They made many friends both in the student body and among the faculty.

His final year of school went quickly. Yohannes was given his first call to a Lutheran Church–Missouri Synod (LCMS) congregation. Yohannes was in consideration to be a "missionary at large" in Texas, where he would be in charge of helping a community of African immigrants with their transitional needs. This was what Yohannes wanted for his first call; this was exactly the type of work he felt the Lord had been preparing him for.

But in the meantime, President Heins of the Michigan District of the LCMS was in need of an associate pastor for Zion Lutheran Church in Holland, Michigan. It was a risk to assign Yohannes to this position. He was fresh from the seminary, but moreover, he would be the first African to be a member of this white, suburban congregation. Yohannes was worried. Would the community accept him? Would he be able to meet their needs? Out of fear, Yohannes insisted on a different assignment from the Council of Presidents, which had the responsibility for assigning seminary graduates. He continued to request a missionary-at-large position where he could serve the Eritreans. But he was denied.

"Yohannes, this is a significant congregation in my district," President Heins told him. "I am trusting you with them. You can do this, I promise," he said.

Yohannes prayed about his assignment. Zion Lutheran was a strong congregation of about 375 people. Besides being the only African in the congregation, he would be the first African clergyperson in Holland, Michigan. The feelings of trepidation and isolation he'd previously experienced in New York City were creeping up on him once again. This would be a sure test of his will and determination. At least this time he wouldn't be alone; he'd have his wife and two sons. Yohannes graduated from Concordia Seminary and accepted the assignment.

CHAPTER 11

Who Will Convert Whom?

HOLLAND, MICHIGAN, IS A COASTAL city along the eastern shore of Lake Michigan. The city is best known for its Dutch heritage. May's Tulip Time Festival and themed attractions such as the Dutch Village, the Settlers' House Museum, and the Cappon House Museum draw thousands of tourists each year.

The now "Pastor" Mengsteab thought the city beautiful, rich in its culture, and alive in its faith. When he arrived with his family, the *Holland Sentinel* published an article about him and his mission at Zion Lutheran Church. Every Sunday Yohannes assisted Pastor Beowulf with worship services while Yohannes's wife and children sat in the pews with the rest of the congregation. At first, the congregation struggled with Yohannes's accent, as his pronunciation wasn't very clear to them. But after a short time, the congregation became as enamored with him as he was with them, and his accent was no longer a problem.

So many wonderful things happened at Zion Lutheran Church while Yohannes served as the associate pastor there. The community celebrated its hundredth year as a congregation in 1993. One of their affluent congregants donated a building to the church in order to build a preschool, which quickly became quite successful within the Holland community. Yohannes helped form a Vacation Bible School program that boasted enrollment of a hundred to a hundred fifty children each time it took place. The church also sponsored a harvest festival that was not only fun for the congregants of the church, but also invited the surrounding community to engage with the church.

Yohannes's responsibility as associate pastor involved not only the youth programs, but also evangelism. He had a goal of recruiting seventy new congregants per year. He worked very hard with families so that their children could be baptized, with the children who were working on their confirmation, and with parishioners who had recently transferred into the church from other congregations. Yohannes made it his goal to respond to every inquiry into the church within seventy-two hours. He liked to meet with people in their homes, where the potential congregant would feel most comfortable and receptive.

One day, one of the church's faithful congregants approached Yohannes.

"Reverend," she began. "My husband is an atheist." Yohannes was surprised to hear this. The woman before him was one of the more devout within his congregation. It was hard for him to imagine that she would be married to an atheist. However, when he thought about it, he did not recall ever seeing her husband attend worship with her.

"I've tried for years to help him see the light," she continued. "Reverend Beowulf and Reverend Hoesman before him tried to help him return to his Christian roots, but he's always been resistant, and it didn't work. Would you please try?"

Yohannes could not resist this challenge. He remembered what it felt like when he renounced his own faith on the battlefield in Eritrea so many years ago. He still remembered how empty and unfulfilled he was during that time, how his life seemed to flounder and he couldn't find much satisfaction from anything.

The first night Yohannes visited his congregant and her husband in their home, she sat him in the living room on the couch and left

Yohannes and her husband alone. (We will call the husband and the congregant Adam and Eve for the sake of this story.)

"Try to convert me," Adam said with a look in his eye that told Yohannes he had his work cut out for him.

"Let's see who converts whom," Yohannes responded. A smirk formed on the atheist's face, growing ever wider and culminating in a chuckle.

"Fair enough, young man," Adam said, still smiling.

Yohannes visited "Adam and Eve's" home every two days after that. Over the course of several meetings, Yohannes learned that Adam had been raised in the Episcopal Church. As he grew into a man, he saw the turn the Episcopal Church was taking: it had accepted a more liberal ideology, which did not sit well with Adam. He decided to leave the church and take his chances out on his own.

In the 1960s Adam became familiar with Communist ideologies. He strove to learn all he could about Communism and its tenets, and he began looking at the world much differently than he had before. He decided that God couldn't possibly exist, and that is when he became a devoted atheist.

During one of their meetings, the man asked for Yohannes's input. He wanted to know about Yohannes and the world that he came from. Yohannes did not hesitate to tell his story. He talked about his crisis of faith while he was part of the ELF. He told him of the Episcopal church in New York City he'd tried to become part of and the Lutheran church he did join. Yohannes talked about the foolishness of materialism, about how its temptation is the trickery of the devil himself trying to push us away from Jesus.

He told Adam how the Lord provides us with everything we need in the world; he provides us the materials to build a home, animals and plants to eat, fire to keep warm and cook our food, and water to drink and bathe in. Cars, radios, televisions, and fancy fashions are all manmade things, and collecting those things doesn't make us happy. It is the things that come from God, especially His love for us and our love for one another, that make us truly happy and rich.

Adam was very quiet after hearing this. He held his head low. Then he said, "Who am I to deny what many wise men before me have believed? Thank you, Reverend." His voice was barely above a whisper.

"Can we pray together?" Yohannes asked, reaching out his hands. Adam looked up and clasped Yohannes's hands tightly.

"I am ready, Reverend," he said. And they prayed together.

The next day Yohannes received word that Adam had passed away.

Eve asked if Yohannes would preside over her husband's funeral. He could not say no. Yohannes was moved to tears by this old man's conversion. For so long this man had been missing Jesus Christ in his life. And finally, once he accepted Jesus, the Lord brought Adam home to sit with Him at the Lord's banquet table, forever.

Yohannes realized that despite the fact that he'd resisted his calling to Zion Lutheran Church in favor of the work a missionary at large would do, the Lord had made this choice for Yohannes. It would have been an easy mission for Yohannes if he had received the assignment to work with the Eritrean refugees, people whose struggles he could understand. But the Lord sent him to Holland, Michigan, to help him understand the American mind-set more fully. God had ordained that Yohannes would be the right missionary to bring an American man to faith, in answer to the prayers of a faithful, loving wife.

CHAPTER 12

The Eritrean
Missionary Society

IN APRIL 1993 A REFERENDUM supported by Ethiopia gave Eritrea the opportunity to vote for its independence. This was a long time in coming, but everyone knew it was inevitable.

In 1991 the Eritrean People's Liberation Front had defeated the Ethiopian military forces stationed in Eritrea. A rebel faction in Ethiopia that was opposed to the government's Marxist regime worked with the EPLF to overthrow the ruling government over Ethiopia and Eritrea. This led to the drafting of the referendum to separate Eritrea from Ethiopia.

In an overwhelming landslide vote, 99 percent of the Eritrean people voted for and were finally granted their independence. On May 28, 1993, the United Nations formally accepted Eritrea into its membership, thereby cementing Eritrea's place as an independent country.

Shortly after Eritrea's independence was announced, Yohannes and his family went to visit family and friends there. Most of the family now had the opportunity to meet Yohannes and Alemash's two young sons for the first time. The homecoming was short, but the celebration went on and on.

When the Mengsteab family returned to Holland, Michigan, Yohannes learned that Pastor Beowulf had left the congregation. With a pastor position to fill, the Michigan District needed to act immediately to begin the call process to replace Pastor Beowulf, who was the fourth pastor to leave the position in six years. The Michigan District decided that it would fill the pastor position, but there would no longer be an associate pastor to work alongside the lead pastor. The Michigan District asked Yohannes to take this lead pastor position. The congregation supported Yohannes's transition to lead pastor, but after much prayer Yohannes turned down the position.

Yohannes had gone to a seminar in Washington, DC, conducted by a Sudanese pastor from Philadelphia. The Lutheran Brotherhood Insurance Company had granted the Southeastern District of the LCMS fifty thousand dollars to reach out to the Eritrean refugee population in Washington, DC. The Southeastern District leadership wanted to provide the refugees with resources they'd need to assimilate into life in the United States. Other programs for the same purpose were also being funded in Houston and Los Angeles. This was exactly the type of position Yohannes was looking for.

When the call came to him, Yohannes was eager to accept the position in Washington, DC, a position that he was granted. Many of the congregants of the parish in Holland were disappointed that Yohannes would be leaving. They'd come to care for him as much as he cared for them, and they would miss him. One congregant was particularly upset that Yohannes would be leaving and begged him to stay. Yohannes had a frank conversation with him.

"There are plenty of people who can fill the pastor position here at Zion Lutheran, but this new position requires qualifications that are unique. My background and experience perfectly fit what is needed to be successful in ministering to an African congregation," he said. Yohannes said he'd remain the solitary pastor in the Zion Lutheran

Church in Holland until a replacement was named. Then he'd begin his journey to Washington, DC.

The Southeastern District sent a moving company to Holland to help the Mengsteab family pack up their belongings and make their way back to the East Coast. Yohannes was eager to begin his new mission, and so was Alemash. She was grateful for the love she had been shown by the congregation in Holland. Although she had met some wonderful women in Holland and would miss her new American friends, her limited English still was a barrier to her fully acclimating. She was eager to integrate into the Eritrean community around Washington, DC; she wished to meet women who spoke her language, cooked the foods she cooked, and knew the stories and history that she knew. Also, she knew that the work Yohannes would be doing was essential—in particular, carrying out his dream to begin an Eritrean Mission Society. This society would bring together leaders in the Eritrean community to discern needs of the people and find ways to meet those needs. The society would open doors to bring those Eritreans who had lost their way back into the church.

A cousin church body to the LCMS, the Evangelical Lutheran Church in America (ELCA), supported Yohannes by providing him and his family an available parsonage in Alexandria, Virginia. The house would be free of charge for six months while the family adapted to their new roles in a new city. This act of kindness eventually allowed the Mengsteab family to save enough money to purchase their own home in Beltsville, Maryland, near the University of Maryland. Beltsville was a family-friendly community, full of children for six-year-old Samson and four-year-old Paulus to play with. They were enrolled in a Lutheran school, found many friends, and adjusted quickly. Yohannes would work out of Redeemer Lutheran Church in Hyattsville, Maryland.

Redeemer Church was large. While most congregants were Anglo-Saxon, there were a number of Ethiopian, Nigerian, and Eritrean members. These were the members Yohannes was to minister to. Part of his responsibility was to evangelize the African populace and bring them into the parish. The pastor of the parish, who was called to another congregation just before Yohannes's arrival, had not been able to serve all the needs of the recent immigrant African population in his church. Many Ethiopians were left spiritually starved, as this pastor did not have the knowledge or resources to tend to their needs properly. Because the former pastor could not overcome cultural and language barriers, many Ethiopian immigrants had become disappointed and left the church.

Yohannes took this call very seriously and strove to repair the relationship between these newly integrated immigrants and Redeemer Church. He visited each African congregant in his or her home. He asked these congregants who else they knew who might have an interest joining Redeemer. They would give him a few names, and Yohannes would reach out. Yohannes felt that it wasn't a hard sell to bring many of these immigrants into the fold of the parish. In many cases Yohannes knew the extended family of the person he was evangelizing. And at the very least, Yohannes was able to relate to the Coptic tradition many of these potential congregants still retained.

Yohannes would go into their homes, share his message, pray with the families, and preach. Before long, the second Sunday service at Redeemer was about 50 percent African, thanks to the vision of the Southeastern District, the commitment of the people of Redeemer, and the dedication of Yohannes to his people.

Out of all these efforts, and with the guidance of God's Holy Spirit, the Eritrean Mission Society became a reality. As a consequence of forming the society, opportunities to help other parishes in the area sprang up. Yohannes served many congregations in the DC and Baltimore area. Among them were Peace Lutheran Church, Our Savior (an all-Eritrean congregation), Lamb of God (a Liberian congregation), and Silver Springs Calvary (a primarily African congregation). Yohannes was able to bridge the cultural and language barriers that existed in these parishes and bring a new depth of faith to the African immigrants with whom he was working. There was an unused house on the property of Peace Lutheran that had once been a parsonage. The congregation agreed that this should be offered as temporary housing for the newly integrated African immigrants to help them get on their feet and begin their new journey.

Like at Redeemer in Hyattsville, Yohannes learned of connections that many of the immigrants he served had to other African immigrant congregants in America and to faithful Christians in Eritrea. Some of them were descendants of already established church members. Others were family of the founding missionaries from Eritrea and Ethiopia, related to the ruling class in Ethiopia. One of the immigrants Yohannes ministered to was the wife of the press secretary for Haile Selassie.

But while the great number of African immigrants was inspiring and provided Yohannes with a great amount of satisfying work, he was aware of the political turmoil that stirred underneath the good deeds taking place around him.

CHAPTER 13

Betrayal

THE POLITICAL CLIMATE HAD CHANGED in Eritrea and Ethiopia. While Eritrea celebrated its independence with joy, with the change also came conflict. The new government was authoritarian, controlling the communities at large. Missionaries in Eritrea were considered suspect and became controversial; in contrast, religious freedom blossomed in Ethiopia. Different political groups in both countries vied for power. The politics and rivalries in Eritrea and Ethiopia produced similar conflicts among the refugee communities in the United States.

To deal with the rivalries among the US refugees, Yohannes made it a policy to never start any ministry without identifying a leader from within the ranks of the newly forming church. In many cases this worked, but in others there was still ethnic and cultural divisions among the new congregants.

Some Eritrean community leaders questioned Yohannes about the money the Southeastern District had provided to support the Eritrean Missionary Society. They felt the money was being used incorrectly, that it should support the Eritreans only and no other African groups. They thought that since Yohannes was Eritrean, his influence should allow the money to be used only to support the Eritreans. "You are keeping this money for yourself," they claimed. Yohannes tried to explain that the grant was specifically to reach all African immigrants, not just Eritreans.

These Eritreans, not satisfied with Yohannes's answer, jumped to a conclusion. They accused Yohannes of misuse of funds.

"My friends, my allegiance is to Jesus Christ, not to the Eritreans. This money given by the Lutheran Brotherhood is for the benefit of all African immigrants, not just a few. Please understand that," Yohannes begged.

But some of the Eritreans found that understanding difficult. To put it into perspective, we might imagine a situation where one leader—for example, someone from the United States—was designated to serve all of North and South America using a lump sum set aside to support the immigrants of all of the countries on the American continents. Citizens from the United States would probably assume that the leader would have the United States' interests at heart first and foremost, and would assume the leader's total loyalty to the United States. Other countries, such as Mexico, with whom the United States has had a checkered past, might assume their needs weren't being considered at all, and if they were, they certainly weren't being given equal support.

Such was true of the Ethiopian and Eritrean communities Yohannes was trying to serve. There were rivalries, rivalries that reached back to Africa.

Despite Yohannes's best attempts to help them understand that his efforts and the money he was given were equally spent, some of the Eritrean leaders did not support Yohannes ministering to anyone else. Their disapproval went so far as to include ostracizing Yohannes's family at church. The Eritreans isolated Yohannes's sons and Alemash, forcing them to listen to unfounded accusations about Yohannes and how he embezzled the funds that had been given to him by the Lutheran Brotherhood to support Eritrean immigrants by using them on refugees from other countries.

Alemash was hurt and angry at the betrayal of the very people she had so hoped to befriend. At first, cultural and language barriers had prevented her from feeling at home in America. Now her own people were making unfounded accusations against her husband, someone who had only the purest of intentions and who had dedicated himself to their service.

"My love," Yohannes said to his beautiful wife. "The devil tries to distract, but the power of the Holy Spirit is strong and will overcome." She held these words close to her heart and believed their power. They helped her to hold her head high when someone in the congregation would sneer at her or abruptly move away from her.

As the rumblings over the rumors that Yohannes had misused funds grew stronger, Yohannes recognized that he needed to be proactive in order to stop this nonsense from marring his reputation in the community as well as the Southeast District. Yohannes sent letters to each of the Eritrean members of both Redeemer and Peace Churches to clear the air. If their goal was to ruin Yohannes's ministry, he would have to engage them in dialogue, face-to-face, as the Bible says should happen (Matthew 18:15). He asked them to ask questions and to look at his books; he would keep all dialogue open and transparent to prove to them he was not misappropriating any funds earmarked for Eritrean progress.

While this satisfied many who'd questioned Yohannes's ministry, one Eritrean was not at all satisfied. He spearheaded a movement against Yohannes and would not be deterred. This man's insinuations were so strong that one of the American pastors at Redeemer Lutheran, Pastor Rudy Kampia, invited Yohannes, the accuser, and any Eritrean congregant who wished to come to an open forum for discussion about the accusations against Yohannes.

"He calls himself a minister," the accuser ranted in front of the attending congregants and Pastor Kampia. "But he's taking the money sent to him for the Eritreans and putting it in his own pocket. It is not coming to us. We've seen none of it!" The accusations and insults went on for nearly thirty minutes before Yohannes had the opportunity to address those in attendance.

By this time Yohannes was deeply hurt. Now the accusations were in the open. He was being accused face-to-face, in front of many people, some from his own congregation. What hurt Yohannes the most was that there were several people in attendance with whom he'd spent long hours in their homes encouraging them and praying with them—people whom he had personally helped get jobs or their driver's licenses, or whom he'd helped find economic stability. Some of those people now stared at him with angry eyes, believing the lies.

"My friends," Yohannes began, "you have my word that nothing I did with the funds I was entrusted with was improper. I used each cent for the purpose it was intended: to assist African immigrants as needed among four parishes. This is what I have done. I've helped you to get jobs, provided you meals, provided you shelter, provided you spiritual counseling. I've done all of that for you, and for the Ethiopians, and the Liberians, and any other African immigrant who demonstrated need. As a servant of Christ, my job is to provide to all, not just a few. And I've done that.

"If you feel I've not done my job properly, if I've not served the community well, then I am sorry. If I've done anything to wrong any of you, I am sorry and I beg your forgiveness. If I've been too busy serving the needs of others and have not served your needs, please forgive me and please grant me the opportunity to right that wrong. But please know, I've done all I can to do my best to serve each and every one of you. Please, speak up and let me know what more I can do."

Yohannes looked expectantly at the people gathered at Redeemer that night, waiting for someone to speak up, for those who he'd wronged to tell him about it. The group remained still and silent. No one spoke up.

At that moment Yohannes was afraid that his mission was being marred by the accusations; he was afraid he would not to be able to do any further constructive work with this group of Eritreans. But as it turned out, no Eritrean got up and left the meeting that night. The faces of the people changed—from anger to thoughtfulness. Soon Pastor Kampia and Yohannes began to realize that the assembly understood that he was innocent and that these accusations were politically motivated. But, still, that night none of the people spoke up to defend him. Perhaps they were afraid of political isolation or repercussions. It didn't matter to Yohannes, so long as his name was cleared. It took years, but the trust that had been broken was eventually healed and friendships were restored.

CHAPTER 14

Lutheran Church–
Missouri Synod

WHEN THE LITANY OF ACCUSATIONS began, Pastor Mengsteab asked the Southeastern District to redistribute his salary, using part of the money to fund part-time work by four local African immigrant leaders. By this time, he himself was beginning to receive part-time support from the national church body. The African Immigrant Task Force wanted Yohannes to start new missions across the country, not just in the Southeastern District. This task force would reach all African immigrants, including but not restricted to Eritreans and Ethiopians. Among other task force members, he recruited Rev. Dr. Doug Rutt, mission professor at Concordia Theological Seminary in Fort Wayne, Indiana, and Professor Will Schumacher of Concordia Seminary, Saint Louis. Both had been overseas missionaries—Rutt in South America and Schumacher in Africa. The three men worked together to write a paper describing the task force's goals and the need for its teaching and recruitment of African immigrants for the two seminaries.

Their goal was to begin seventy new African immigrant ministries across the nation. To accomplish this, they knew that they needed right away to anticipate the need for African leaders in communities heavily populated with new immigrants. Leaders should be equipped to serve the needs of the immigrants properly and immediately. Because the immigrants from different countries had different needs, it would be underserving these communities to put African immigrants under one all-encompassing umbrella. Individual cohorts of immigrants from different cultures needed to be created. Most immigrants would be more receptive to someone from their own background leading them. Some of the education for these leaders could come through the seminaries.

Yohannes and his group approached the Lutheran Church–Missouri Synod (LCMS), the second-largest body of the Lutheran Church in the United States (after the Evangelical Lutheran Church in America, or ELCA), about the idea for an African Immigrant Institute of Theology. On the board sat Dr. Robert Scudieri, head of national mission work for the LCMS. Scudieri immediately got behind this effort. He asked Yohannes to head up a national task force that would include leaders who had immigrated to America from any African country. Annual meetings would be held right at the LCMS's International Center in Saint Louis.

The creation of the African Immigrant Task Force was a huge step forward for mission work in the United States. But then challenges started arising. The old ways were not going to help grow the mission field.

Opposition arose to creating a seminary training program for the immigrants, something that at the time was called the "African Immigrant Institute of Theology," or AIIT for short. For one thing, the board of the African Immigrant Task Force questioned the possibility of one seminary that would serve the many different cultures of the mission fields from which leaders could be cultivated. There were too many cultures to serve.

Another barrier raised by some was that there was already a program up and running at the seminaries called "Distance Education Leading to Ordination" (DELTO). The seminaries felt an African Immigrant

Institute of Theology would be too similar to what DELTO was proposing. African students interested in becoming pastors—like any students who felt called to ministry—could benefit from DELTO and not have to move to Saint Louis or Fort Wayne (and therefore not have to sell their homes and uproot their families). DELTO was meant not just to save money for the students, but these programs also allowed the students to learn in their cultural settings the things unique to their culture.

Yohannes became gravely discouraged. Without a more open way to ordain new immigrant leaders, he knew progress in growing African immigrant churches would be stopped in its tracks. DELTO, he felt, was too restrictive. The students needed to be thirty-five years old, have been Lutheran for ten years, and have had completed two years of college already. A viable immigrant program could not find that kind of student in numbers large enough to meet the needs of a growing mission field in the United States. But the seminaries insisted that a duplicate program like AIIT would never be agreed to or funded according to the bylaws of the LCMS.

Supporters of the AIIT approach insisted the DELTO program was unrealistic. A general education would not properly prepare any individual for handling specific ethnic groups; groups of people are not "one size fits all." The education must be much more geared toward the community that would be served. Doug Rutt, the representative from Fort Wayne who had helped Yohannes with the paper outlining the task force's goals, mentioned that the Fort Wayne seminary had a program specifically to support the Haitian population, so this had been done already. Why couldn't a program be designed for African immigrants?

Professor Cameron McKenzie of Fort Wayne, a board member sitting in during this debate, took it a step further. He exposed a loophole in the bylaws that stated a specialized ministry can develop specialized theology studies and be established in institutes as such. This certainly proved a distinct difference between the AIIT and the generic DELTO program!

With this new information supporting their cause, the group of leaders went to President Johnson at the Saint Louis seminary and presented their case.

"Gentlemen," he said, "I thank you for bringing this to my attention. I'll admit, we've not been really good at reaching out to multiethnic communities and addressing the diversities among our congregants. You have my blessing. Now, convince the faculty."

Eagerly, the AIIT supporters addressed the Board for Higher Education, proposing their plan. One member, Andrew Bartelt, was a terrific supporter of the program. He worked the networks within the seminary and other educational channels to convince the faculty at Saint Louis of the need for such a program. After some debate the board decided that the AIIT supporters' aim would be best served if the institute became the EIIT, or Ethnic Immigrant Institute of Theology, so as to encompass the needs of immigrants of all nations. The Lord gave the mission leaders more than they could ever have expected.

The program was accepted and is still in effect today. The LCMS, through its partnering seminaries in Saint Louis and Fort Wayne, offers the EIIT program. It has evolved into a state-of-the-art online education program that provides theological education for effective leadership within multicultural and immigrant-based congregations.

While Yohannes had always been determined and knew that if he put his mind to something, he could do it, he recognized that often there had to be someone there holding the door open for the leaders of the new mission fields being started by immigrants. For Yohannes, this gift came from Dr. Bob Scudieri. And Dr. Scudieri's role in Yohannes's life had just begun.

CHAPTER 15

Who Are We to Judge?

REV. YOHANNES MENGSTEAB, STILL A missionary in the Southeastern District, embraced his new adventures as the chairman of the national African Immigrant Task Force. The Saint Louis seminary launched its ethnic immigrant program immediately. Yohannes's responsibilities included identifying people to attend the new institute. He wanted to find leaders who could create other leaders to keep the program constantly growing, thus propelling the mission forward and expanding the church through leadership development. His first step was to find key leaders in the largest and most affected urban areas in the eastern and midwestern areas of the United States. Soon districts in the western part of the country eagerly joined in.

With the expansion of African immigrant mission work nationwide, the board of the African Immigrant Task Force officially asked Dr. Bob Scudieri, the head of national missions, to agree that Yohannes be made a member of the national mission staff. New African immigrant congregations were being developed rapidly and in many other areas of the country. Dr. Scudieri readily agreed.

With Dr. Scudieri's encouragement and the decision of the Saint Louis seminary to begin the EIIT, Yohannes accepted the call of the LCMS Board for Missions and moved his family from Washington, DC, to Saint Louis. Not too long afterward a third son entered the Mengsteab household: little Mebratu.

Yohannes received much support from many districts of the LCMS, including Texas, where Rev. Ken Hennings was the mission executive; the Pacific Northwest, whose mission executive was Ken Behnken; and Ohio, whose mission executive was Rev. Dick Gahl. Yohannes's heart swelled with joy that the EIIT had been well received and was supported by many districts.

One of Yohannes's highlights during this period was when he had the opportunity to spend time with the Native American ministry. Yohannes was asked to attend a tribal council for Native Americans. He was surprised to see only two Native American pastors present; the rest were Anglo-Saxon.

"Why are there so few Native American pastors present?" he asked incredulously.

"We were unable to find someone appropriate to lead," one of the Anglo pastors replied.

Immediately, Yohannes became upset. How was it possible that of an entire population of people, so few could be qualified to lead? Yohannes found this difficult to believe and turned to the EIIT.

At the time the EIIT didn't serve the Native American population, but because Yohannes had brought the need to their attention, the EIIT saw the need and readily responded, adding Native Americans to the ethnic groups invited to participate. They reached out to Native American populations, looking for applicants. Many applied and began to go through the vetting process. Yohannes was asked to be part of that process, and he happily agreed.

One man who came to apply was quickly rejected by many who interviewed him.

"Why are we being so quick to dismiss this man?" Yohannes asked.

"He's had multiple marriages," said one staff member.

"And alcohol issues," said another.

"Did he have these problems before he was Christian?" Yohannes asked.

One staff member scanned the paperwork. "It appears so," she said.

"Well, what do you expect from a non-Christian?" Yohannes asked. "The apostle Paul was a murderer before he began following the words of Christ and became an apostle. If Jesus can look beyond the mistakes someone makes before following Him and His teachings, then who are we to judge a man based on his life before Christ?" After Yohannes took up his case, this man's application was approved.

Due to the EIIT, there are now more Native American pastors serving Native American churches than ever before. This is only one example among many that illustrates the power of the EIIT and how important its role is in mission fields of the United States.

The die had been cast. Now a strategy was in place for providing immigrants the access they needed to grow their mission fields. Was there anything more that could be done?

CHAPTER 16

Critical Moments
Shape Our Lives

YOHANNES'S MINISTRY IS STILL ONGOING. Alemash has become a joyful member of American society with many friends and satisfaction from her volunteer work. The two older boys, Samson and Paulus, have gone on to college. Mebratu is at home, a joy to his mother and father.

Yohannes says the missionary's heart must be resilient due to the interference it faces from Satan every day. He likes to say, "The devil works hard to destroy those in mission service." In a recent interview recorded for this book Yohannes said, "It is important to the devil to discourage missionaries so that the love of Christ will be kept from people. The more people who are brought to Christ, the less room there is for Satan. So Satan must find ways to tempt or discourage missionaries so they'll stop their work. I will never stop."

Imagine if the Swedish missionaries had been discouraged by the warring factions along the Ethiopian border and headed home through the Red Sea. What if they'd decided to cut their losses and go back to Sweden?

Imagine if Yohannes had opted to remain in the refugee camp in the Sudan, afraid of what would happen if he left Africa for a strange and foreign land. What if he'd ignored God's call to him to leave his comfortable life in Holland, Michigan, to go to the cities of the southeastern United States? When would all of the Liberians, Eritreans, Ethiopians, and Americans who were looking for hope and faith have found what they were looking for? A missionary's journey is wrought with challenges, dramatic changes, and sometimes failures. But what makes the heart of a missionary so strong is that missionaries are determined in their call, courageous in their journey, and always resilient.

Yohannes believes life brings critical moments that shape our being and determine where we are going. He looks back to Eritrea, when he was indoctrinated into the ELF, as one of those moments. Had he remained in Eritrea and not fled to the Swedish missionary-led refugee camp in the Sudan, he doubts his faith would be part of his life at all.

If he hadn't been injured in the war for independence in Eritrea, he most likely would have stayed with the Communist Party and discarded his Christian faith permanently. He doubts he would have reidentified with Christianity if he had become a political leader.

In Eritrea today, church leadership is generally reserved for those without great academic ability, so because of his intelligence, Yohannes wouldn't have been driven toward the church in any way.

Yohannes believes leaving Eritrea wasn't entirely his choice. He feels he was pushed to leave because it was God's will and because of the political climate in Eritrea. He didn't support the ruling political party, so that was a factor in his choice to flee to the refugee camp. And through that, his passion to preach the words of Christ was initiated.

Perhaps Yohannes's words say it best of all: "There is no greater wealth than the grace of God and to be called to spread His word to everyone who will listen."

If one life can be changed, one life impacted, one life given hope, and one life led to faith, these results are worth the hard work, sacrifice, and yes, even the suffering that a missionary must undergo.

Every person who has accomplished something significant in life has done it on the shoulders of someone else. It is the will of God that brings us all together, and in some way, we all contribute to one another's journey and God's plan for us. Many of the people who have assisted in Yohannes's journey have been mentioned in these pages. But there are still many others who have significantly helped Yohannes along the way through their dedication and generosity and who have given him the stability he needed to blossom into the spiritual leader he is today.

There are more such missionaries to America, and they face the same challenges faced by Yohannes Mengsteab. They have been discouraged, they have had to sacrifice in order to continue missionary work, and they have experienced miracles in their ministry and found the strength to go on. These missionaries are gifts from God.

About the Author

CHRISTINE SCHULDEN GRADUATED FROM LaSALLE University with a bachelor's degree in communications, focusing on journalism and public relations, and two minors in art history and English literature. Upon graduation, Schulden worked as a producer at a sports and talk radio station in Philadelphia before transitioning into the role of traffic coordinator.

Schulden then turned her love of television into a new career opportunity, taking a job as a media buyer for a Philadelphia-based agency. There, she honed her marketing skills and bought television and radio advertising space for many clients across the nation.

Despite her background in radio and television, Schulden has always been a novelist at heart, earning admission to the Institute For Children's Literature at age twelve. Since then, she's spent her life developing plots and creating characters.

She lives in New Jersey with her wonderful husband, their three amazing little ladies, two cats, and several fish.

Made in the USA
Columbia, SC
07 November 2018